B Recipe Cookbook

Healthy Smoothie, Soup and Dessert Recipes for your High Speed Blender

By
Jesse Morgan

LEGAL

Copyright © 2015 – Stone River Solutions, LLC. All rights reserved.

No part of this book may be reproduced, stored in a retrieval system, or transmitted, in any form or by any means, electronic or photocopy or otherwise, without the prior written permission of the publisher except in the case of brief quotations within critical articles and reviews. You must not circulate this book in any format. This book is licensed for your personal enjoyment only. The ebook version may not be resold or given away to other people.

Although the author and publisher have made every effort to ensure that the information in this book was correct at press time, the author and publisher do not assume and hereby disclaim any liability to any party for any loss, damage, or disruption caused by errors or omissions, whether such errors or omissions result from negligence, accident, or any other cause.

The author/ publisher is not engaged in rendering legal, accounting, medical or other professional services. The information and opinions presented in this book are intended for informational purposes only.

TABLE OF CONTENTS

Legal 2

Introduction 6

Chapter 1: Health Benefits of Juicing 8
    What are the Health Benefits of Juices
    and Smoothies? 8
    Getting the Most Out of Your High-Speed Blender 10
    Choosing Your Ingredients Wisely 12
    Using Your Blender for Weight Loss and Fitness 13

Chapter 2: A Comparison of Different Types of Blenders .. 15
    What to Look for in a High-Speed Blender 15
    Top-Performing High-Speed Blender Brands 18
    The Bottom Line 20

SMOOTHIES 22
    Raspberry Almond Smoothie 23
    Cherries Jubilee Smoothie 24
    Green Spa Smoothie 25
    Fruity Breakfast Smoothie 26
    Carrot Caribbean Smoothie 27
    Superfood Pomegranate Smoothie 28
    Lemon Drop Smoothie 29
    Blueberry Pie Smoothie 30

Watermelon Cooler 31
Chocolate Covered Strawberry Smoothie.................... 32
Chilly Cappaccino Breakfast Smoothie......................... 33
Banana Date Smoothie: 34
Creamy Green Avocado Smoothie: 35
Get You Going Smoothie... 36
Ruby Raspberry Smoothie 37

SOUP **38**
Loaded Potato Soup.. 39
Spicy Tomatillo Soup with Chicken 41
Roasted Red Pepper Soup 42
Sweet Potato Bisque 44
Black Bean Soup... 45
Carrot Ginger Soup 46
Broccoli Cheddar Soup.. 47
Chicken Tortilla Soup 48
Roasted Butternut Squash Soup 50
Cantaloupe Gazpacho... 52
Easy Tomato Basil Soup 53
Potato Leek Soup.. 55
Fresh Corn Chowder 57
Creamy Pea Soup.. 58
Quick Pumpkin Soup 59

DESSERTS... **60**
Fresh Mint Chocolate Chip Ice Cream........................... 61
Easy Chocolate Raspberry Mousse 63
Hydrating Kiwi Sorbet 64

Vanilla and Green Tea Ice Cream 65
Ginger Peach Frozen Yogurt 66
Pina Colada Ice Cream 67
Orange Sorbet 69
Watermelon Lime Granita...........................71
Strawberry Frozen Yogurt 72
Homemade Strawberry Sauce.....................73
Blueberry Lemon Pound Cake 74
Banana Soft Serve Ice Cream......................76
Mango Chili Pops..77
Coconut Lime Sorbet 78
Homemade Healthy Truffles 79

INTRODUCTION

Hello and thank you for purchasing my latest book.

I have owned a number of blenders in the past. I recently purchased a Vitamix blender and quickly began to experiment in creating new smoothie, soup and dessert recipes. My original plan was to title this book Vitamix Blender Recipes. I contacted the Vita-mix corporation and found that they do not allow the use of their brand names in the titles of books, which is why I went with the more generic title. Every recipe in this book has been tested and tasted with a Vitamix blender. Most of the recipes will work fine with other blender brands.

If you have read any of my other books, Carb Cycling: The Recipe & Diet Book or Make Ahead Meals, you will know that my focus is always on healthy nutritious diet conscious meals. Blender recipes make it easy to stay on that path, since the ingredients are mostly fruits and vegetables. That said you still have to be careful with the amount of fruits you use as they are high in sugar and calories.

In the next two chapters, I cover some of the benefits of juicing and then provide some information to help you make a decision on the blender that is right for you, then straight into the recipes.

Please make sure to stop by my site, **www.fitrecipe.net** to sign up for my mailing list. I usually send out free copies of new books to the FitRecipe community in advance of their release. If you have any comments or suggestions, my email address is listed below.

If you find this book of value, please write a quick review on Amazon to share your thoughts with the Amazon community of readers.

Make sure to stop visit **www.fitrecipe.net** to get your free High Speed Blender Buying Guide.

Jesse Morgan – **Jesse@fitRecipe.net**

I am not a nutritionist or a medical practitioner. I love researching topics around nutrition, weight loss and fitness and then sharing that information with others that have similar interests.

CHAPTER 1: HEALTH BENEFITS OF JUICING

What if I told you that you could receive almost your entire day's worth of fruits and vegetables just by drinking a 16-ounce glass of juice. I am not talking about the kind of juice you can buy in a carton at the grocery store – I am talking about nutritious, fresh-squeezed juice that you can make at home. Juicing is one of the hottest current health and fitness trends, and for good reason. A glass of fresh-squeezed juice contains dozens of healthy nutrients all in one delicious and easy-to-digest package. If you have never tried juicing before, I would encourage you to give it a try. Before getting into the details of juicing, however, I would like to tell you what makes juicing so great.

What are the Health Benefits of Juices and Smoothies?

If you are trying to lose weight or simply improve your health, the first thing you need to do is improve your diet. The modern Western diet is loaded with processed foods, fast food, and fried foods which are all high in calories and relatively low in nutritional value. In order to transform your life, you need to start by changing your diet. By eating whole foods you can fuel your body with the healthy nutrients it needs to maintain proper function –

not only will you find yourself feeling better, but it won't be long before you start looking better too! If you aren't the type of person who enjoys eating large plates of vegetables or if you struggle to work fresh fruit into your daily diet, juices and smoothies may be the solution you've been looking for.

Juicing is an easy and delicious way to work some fruits and vegetables into your daily diet.

Here is just a partial list of the possible benefits of juicing:
- The nutrients contained in fresh-squeezed juice are easy for your body to absorb – this means that they enter your bloodstream quickly because your intestinal tract doesn't need to work hard to break down the whole foods first.
- Fresh juice contains valuable enzymes – cooking fruits and vegetables can destroy those enzymes but, with fresh juice, up to 95% of the enzyme content is preserved.
- Juicing may help to support your weight loss goals because fresh juices can be used as a meal replacement that can be low in calories but rich in nutrition.
- The vital nutrients found in fresh juice may help to support a healthy immune system – juicing on a regular basis may help to lower your risk for serious health problems like heart disease, type 2 diabetes, cancer, and stroke.
- Fresh-squeezed juice has not been pasteurized (the kind of juice you buy at the store typically is), so the vitamin and mineral content is still largely intact.
- Juicing is a valuable tool that complements a variety of healthy diets including anti-inflammatory diets designed

- to combat autoimmune disorders like ulcerative colitis, rheumatoid arthritis, and Crohn's disease.
- Raw juices contain valuable anthocyanins and flavonoids which can help to protect your body against the kind of oxidative cellular damage known to cause neurodegenerative diseases like Alzheimer's and Parkinson's disease.

If the above list of benefits is not enough to convince you of the merits of juicing, consider this: one 16-ounce glass of juice contains as many nutrients as 2 pounds of carrots, or 8 pounds of spinach, or a dozen apples. If you could get almost your entire day's worth of fruits and vegetables by drinking a single glass of juice, wouldn't you do it? If you have a high-speed blender, it is easier than you might think to obtain all of these health benefits and more.

Getting the Most Out of Your High-Speed Blender

Now that you understand the benefits of juicing, you may be curious to know what else your high-speed blender is good for. High-speed blenders are designed to chop, crush, and puree tough ingredients like fresh fruits, whole vegetables, and ice cubes. Not only are these ingredients the core of fresh juices and smoothies, but they can also be used to make fresh soups, dips, desserts, and more. Your high-speed blender is a versatile and powerful tool that can be used to make a wide variety of recipes to support you in your switch to a healthier diet. To give you a better idea what you can do with your blender, consider the following list of foods that you can use in your blend for soups, smoothies, juices, and more:

- Apples
- Arugula
- Beets
- Berries
- Bell peppers
- Cauliflower
- Cantaloupe
- Cherries
- Celery
- Cucumber
- Grapes
- Grapefruit
- Kiwi
- Kale
- Lemon
- Lime
- Mango
- Onions
- Oranges
- Peaches
- Pears
- Pineapple
- Spinach
- Sweet potato
- Tomatoes
- Watermelon
- Zucchini

This is just a sampling of the many fruits and vegetables you can use in your high-speed blender. You can also use fresh herbs, spices, nuts, and seeds. To make the blending of your ingredients easier, you should also use some kind of liquid – healthy options include water, coconut water, unsweetened fruit juice, almond milk, coconut milk, and more. When it comes to making recipes using your high-speed blender, your options are limitless.

Choosing Your Ingredients Wisely

A high-speed blender is one of the most valuable tools in your kitchen because it is so versatile. Even though you can use your blender for almost any ingredient, some ingredients are better than others. When it comes to making healthy recipes using your high-speed blender, I would highly encourage you to go organic. There is a great deal of debate regarding the benefits of organic ingredients and whether they are worth the higher price. I do not expect you to take my word for it that organics are better but I am confident that after I tell you about the differences between organic and non-organic foods that the decision will come naturally to you.

When you go to the grocery store to pick out the ingredients to use in your favorite blender recipes, how do you know which ingredients to pick? When it comes to fruit, you probably select the fruits that are brightly colored, unbruised, and ripe. For leafy green vegetables you look for healthy, crisp leaves with good color. What if I were to tell you that many of the qualities you look for in fresh produce can be manipulated with chemicals? That's right, commercial food manufacturers have the ability to chemically change the color of their foods to make them look more appealing. They also use artificial preservatives to prevent fruits from spoiling and vegetables from bruising. How does it feel to know that you are being lied to every time you walk down the produce aisle?

Now, all of this may seem a little bit extreme to you but I use these examples to help you see the truth. Even the foods that you might consider "safe" because they haven't been processed and packaged can still be riddled with chemicals. Organic foods, on the other hand, are required by law to be free from pesticides, fungicides, insecticides, herbicides, hormones, antibiotics, and artificial ingredients or preservatives. The United States Department of Agriculture (USDA) closely monitors the labeling of organic foods so, if something bears the USDA Organic label, you can rest assured that it is as fresh and as natural as it can be.

Using Your Blender for Weight Loss and Fitness

As I have already mentioned, your high-speed blender is a valuable tool for weight loss and improved nutrition. Many people wrongly assume that going on a diet or trying to improve your health means that you have to buy expensive foods and follow complicated recipes. In reality, the simpler your meals are, the better they are for you. Nothing is simpler, or easier, than throwing a few ingredients in your high-speed blender to make a fresh smoothie or soup. You can even use your blender to make healthy snacks and desserts like pudding, ice cream, dips, and more. If you can imagine it, you can blend it – that is my philosophy, anyway.

The key to success with your weight loss efforts is to ensure that you do not go over your daily calorie allotment and that the calories you do consume provide good nutritional value. For example, while you could eat nothing but candy bars all day and still lose weight (as long as you stay within your calorie restrictions), you probably would not feel very good. All of that sugar and the lack of healthy nutrients would leave you feeling strung out, run down, and downright icky. Using your high-speed blender to make low-calorie soups, smoothies, and snacks, on the other hand, is an easy way to fuel your body with healthy nutrients without going over your daily calorie goals.

If you are serious about losing weight, getting fit, or just improving your health then you should consider investing in a quality high-speed blender. There are many different types of blenders out there including high-capacity blenders, single-serve blenders, and more. Simply put, there is a blender for every need. Once you bring your blender home you will be able to try out some of the delicious and nutritious recipes provided in this book. So what are you waiting for, get shopping!

CHAPTER 2: A COMPARISON OF DIFFERENT TYPES OF BLENDERS

By now it is my hope that you understand the value of having a high-quality blender as part of your kitchen arsenal. Not only can you use your high-speed blender to make fresh juices and smoothies, but you can also use it for homemade soups, dips, snacks, desserts, and more. Your blender is soon to become your best friend and ally in your weight loss efforts and your journey toward improved health and fitness. If you do not already own a high-speed blender, or if you are in the market for a new one, there are many different options to choose from. The blender you select is a matter of preference and it is completely up to you what you decide, but I would like to share my experience with different models to help make your decision a little bit easier.

What to Look for in a High-Speed Blender

Before I get into the specifics regarding certain blender brands, it is important that you know what to look for in a high-speed blender. A high-quality blender does more than just crush ice or make smoothies – it also blends fresh juices, purees soups, and emulsifies homemade dressings. You can use a quality high-speed blender to make everything from smoothies and soups to dips, desserts, and more. When shopping for a blender, the key elements you should consider include the following:

- Motor size/speed
- Container options
- Blade style/material
- Speed settings
- Special features

Motor Size/Speed – The type and size of a blender's motor determines its power. If you intend to use your blender for tough jobs like crushing ice and blending smoothies, you should look for something that offers at least 2 to 3 horsepower. When shopping for a blender, you will also see mentions of motor wattage and peak performance. The wattage simply refers to the amount of electricity the blender consumes while running – a low wattage doesn't necessarily mean low power. More important to consider is the blender's "peak performance" – this is the maximum amount of power available for blending tough ingredients, so you want this number to be as high as possible.

Container Options – High-speed blenders come with a variety of container options. Some blenders are only designed for large-capacity blending while others are specialized for single-serve use. If you plan to blend for the whole family or you want to use your blender for large recipes like soups, choose one with a larger blending container (around 64 fluid ounces is standard). If you want to make single- or double-serve smoothies or blended beverages to take on-the-go, you may want to go with a "personal" blender style that comes with smaller 12-, 16-, or 20-ounce blending cups.

Blade Style/Material – Another important factor to consider when shopping for blenders is the type of blade. Some blenders come with two different types of blade – one for wet blending (liquid) and another for dry blending (grains). A dry blade is designed to help pull ingredients down into the blender – this is important when blending thick recipes like dough. Wet blades, on the other hand, are ideal for blending liquids like smoothies and soups. Some blenders may even come with a multi-function blade which can handle both dry and wet ingredients. The type of blade style you choose will depend on what you intend to use your blender for.

Speed Settings – Different blenders offer different speed settings. Some blenders only have a "high" or "low" power option while others offer a range of 6 or more blending speeds. If you intend to use your blender for a variety of different recipes, you may want to choose something with variable speed controls. If you primarily plan to use your blender for smoothies, look for something with a "crush ice" function or a dedicated "smoothie" pre-programmed setting.

Special Features – In addition to motor, container size, blade style, and speed settings, you should also consider any special features certain blenders offer. A pulse feature, for example, may come in handy for chopping nuts or for breaking down large ingredients prior to blending. The style of lid that comes with the blender is also important to consider – some come with a removable insert that enables you to add ingredients while the blender is running. You should also think about whether the blender components are dishwasher safe and BPA-free.

Top-Performing High-Speed Blender Brands

Now that you have an idea what qualities you should be looking for in a high-speed blender you can start to think about specific brands. Below you will find a list of some of the top-performing blender brands to think about:

Vitamix – When it comes to high-performance blenders, Vitamix is one of the top names in the industry. Available in a variety of different models, Vitamix blenders are designed to provide multi-function blending, capable of handling everything from juices and smoothies to soups, dips, and desserts. These blenders come in large-capacity and single-serve models and not only do they blend, but they offer many of the same functions you would expect from a high-quality food processor like pulsing, chopping, and emulsifying. Vitamix blenders are highly versatile with a variety of pre-programmed settings and variable speed options – they also offer a self-cleaning function.

Ninja – Another popular name in the blender industry is Ninja. Ninja is known for producing professional-grade blenders designed for at-home use. These blenders are available in a variety of sizes ranging from the Nutri Ninja personal blender with single-serve blending cups to the Ninja Ultima which provides 2.5 peak horsepower and 24,000 RPM. Ninja blenders typically offer variable speed settings as well as dedicated pulse and ice crushing options – they also feature unique blade designs which help to ensure a smooth and even blend.

KitchenAid – Not only does KitchenAid product a variety of major appliances, but they also offer several countertop blenders. KitchenAid blenders come in a variety of shapes, sizes, and colors and they are more affordable than some of the professional-grade blenders made by Vitamix and Ninja. One of the most popular KitchenAid blenders is the 5-Speed Classic which features a 5-speed motor and a SoftStart feature which starts the motor at a low speed to draw ingredients into the blade then speeds up for a smooth blend. The new Torrent Magnetic Drive Blender offers a variety of convenient features including pre-set programs for juices, soups, and milkshakes – it also features magnetic drive technology to lock the pitcher in place during blending.

Oster – If variety is the name of the game, Oster is a top-performer. Oster offers a wide variety of blenders including personal blenders, large-capacity blenders, dedicated smoothie blenders, and multi-purpose kitchen blenders. If you do not have a large budget to work with, Oster is a great option. You may not receive some of the more advanced features or the most powerful motor (like you would with Vitamix or Ninja), but Oster blenders are typically pretty good for general purpose blending.

Cuisinart – Another household name in kitchen appliances is Cuisinart. This company produces a variety of mid-range blenders in a number of different sizes. The Velocity Ultra 7.5 1HP Blender offers pre-programmed settings for crushing ice and blending smoothies – it also features a large 56-ounce blending container. The SmartPower Compact Portable Blending/Chopping System is ideal for personal blending, equipped with both a 32-ounce blender jar and four 16-ounce travel cups. Cuisinart also offers several blenders that come with chopping/food processing cups for added versatility.

The Bottom Line

With so many different blenders out there, making a decision can be tough. If you are looking for a high-quality and reliable blender that will last you for many years to come, my personal recommendation is the Vitamix. The Vitamix blender comes in several different models to suit your individual needs and preferences. The S-Series, for example, is a high-performance personal blender that can be used to make single or double servings of your favorite recipes – it also enables you to take your concoctions on the go in a handy to-go cup. The C-Series consists of a variety of sizes all with the classic Vitamix body style. These blenders offer features like variable speed control, pre-programmed blending settings, and large blending containers.

If you like the power and special features provided by the C-Series Vitamix but you do not have a lot of storage space in your kitchen, the G-Series may be a good option for use. These next-generation blenders offer all of the premium blending features for which Vitamix is known in a sleek, low-profile design that fits under your kitchen counter. These blenders still offer high-capacity blending containers as well as variable speed control and pre-programmed blending options. They also come in several different colors to match your kitchen décor. No matter what you plan to use your blender for, it is my opinion that the Vitamix will get the job done each and every time.

Now that you know the basics about high-speed blenders, you should be properly equipped to decide which model is the right choice for you. After you've brought your blender home and set it up, all that is left for you to do is to give it a try! Select one of the delicious recipes I've compiled for you in this book to test out your new blender. Before long, your new high-speed blender will become your favorite kitchen appliance and a valuable tool to support your weight loss and improved health efforts.

SMOOTHIES

Raspberry Almond Smoothie

Makes One Servings

Ingredients:

- 1 cup frozen raspberries
- 1/2 cup 0% fat plain Greek yogurt
- 2 tablespoons almond butter
- 2 medjool dates, pitted
- 1 teaspoon almond extract
- 1 cup skim milk
- 1/2 cup ice

Instructions:

Place all ingredients into your blender and blend on high for 30 seconds, using the paddle to ensure all ingredients are blended smoothly, enjoy!

Benefits:

Raspberries are high in antioxidants. Greek yogurt and skim milk add calcium and protein without any extra fat. Almond butter provides your body with additional protein and healthy fats. Dates provide your smoothie with a blood sugar friendly sweetness and creaminess.

Nutrition:

Calories: 485	Fat: 17g	Carbs: 60g	Protein: 27g

Cherries Jubilee Smoothie

Makes One Servings

Ingredients:

- 1 cup frozen, pitted cherries
- 1 cup 0% fat vanilla Greek yogurt
- 1 cup skim milk
- 2 medjool dates, pitted
- 1/2 cup ice

Instructions:

Place all ingredients into your blender and blend on high for 30 seconds, using the paddle to ensure all ingredients are blended smoothly, enjoy!
*Turn this into a dessert smoothie by adding 1 tablespoon of rum or cognac like the traditional cherries jubilee!

Benefits:

Cherries are a superfood, they are high in antioxidants.

Nutrition:

| Calories: 156 | Fat: 1g | Carbs: 40g | Protein: 2g |

Green Spa Smoothie

Makes One Servings

INGREDIENTS:

- 1 large banana, frozen
- 1/2 cup fresh spinach
- 1/2 cup chopped hot house cucumber
- 4 fresh mint leaves
- 1 cup coconut water

INSTRUCTIONS:

Place all ingredients into your blender and blend on high for 30 seconds, using the paddle to ensure all ingredients are blended smoothly, enjoy!

BENEFITS:

Bananas and coconut water are high in potassium while spinach is high in iron, zinc, and niacin. This smoothie is an all natural multivitamin, perfect for an afternoon pick-me-up.

NUTRITION:

Calories: 387	Fat: 1g	Carbs: 67g	Protein: 33g

Fruity Breakfast Smoothie

Makes One Servings

Ingredients:

- 1 large banana, frozen
- 1 large orange, peeled
- 1/2 cup frozen raspberries
- 1 cup 0% fat vanilla Greek yogurt
- 1 cup skim milk
- 1/2 cup ice

Instructions:

Place all ingredients into your blender and blend on high for 30 seconds, using the paddle to ensure all ingredients are blended smoothly, enjoy!

Benefits:

Bananas are high in potassium and oranges are high in vitamin C. The Greek yogurt and skim milk add calcium and protein to this smoothie without any extra fat.

Nutrition:

Calories: 429	Fat: 1g	Carbs: 78g	Protein: 34g

Carrot Caribbean Smoothie

> Makes One Servings

INGREDIENTS:

- 1 large carrots
- 1/2 cup frozen pineapple
- 1/2 cup frozen mango
- 2 tablespoons dried goji berries
- 1 cup coconut water

INSTRUCTIONS:

Place all ingredients into your blender and blend on high for 30 seconds, using the paddle to ensure all ingredients are blended smoothly, enjoy!

BENEFITS:

Carrots are high in beta-carotene. Goji berries are known as a superfood, they are very high in vitamin A.

NUTRITION:

| Calories: 262 | Fat: 0g | Carbs: 63g | Protein: 7g |

Superfood Pomegranate Smoothie

Makes One Servings

INGREDIENTS:

- 1 cup frozen mixed berries
- 1 cup 0% fat vanilla Greek yogurt
- 1/2 cup pomegranate juice
- 1/2 cup skim milk
- 1/2 cup fresh spinach

INSTRUCTIONS:

Place all ingredients into your blender and blend on high for 30 seconds, using the paddle to ensure all ingredients are blended smoothly, enjoy!

BENEFITS:

Berries and pomegranates are high in antioxidants

NUTRITION:

| Calories: 316 | Fat: 1g | Carbs: 52g | Protein: 28g |

Lemon Drop Smoothie

Makes One Servings

INGREDIENTS:

- ➢ 1 cup 0% fat lemon Greek yogurt
- ➢ 1 cup skim milk
- ➢ 2 teaspoons sugar free lemon Jello mix
- ➢ 1 cup ice

INSTRUCTIONS:

Place all ingredients into your blender and blend on high for 30 seconds, using the paddle to ensure all ingredients are blended smoothly, enjoy!

BENEFITS:

Greek yogurt and skim milk add protein and calcium to this delicious smoothie while keeping it fat free. Sugar free Jello is a great way to add tasty flavor to your smoothies without excess sugar or calories.

NUTRITION:

Calories: 226	Fat: 0g	Carbs: 24g	Protein: 31g

BLUEBERRY PIE SMOOTHIE

Makes One Servings

INGREDIENT:

- 1 cup frozen blueberries
- 1/2 cup 0% fat plain Greek yogurt
- 1 cup skim milk
- 1/4 cup dry oats
- 1 teaspoon cinnamon
- 3 medjool dates

INSTRUCTIONS:

Place all ingredients into your blender and blend on high for 30 seconds, using the paddle to ensure all ingredients are blended smoothly, enjoy!

BENEFITS:

Blueberries are high in vitamin C and K, they are also high in antioxidants. The yogurt and milk are high in protein and calcium and the dates add a blood sugar friendly sweetness.

NUTRITION:

| Calories: 428 | Fat: 2g | Carbs: 84g | Protein: 24g |

Watermelon Cooler

Makes One Servings

INGREDIENTS:

- 1 cup fresh watermelon
- 1 tablespoon frozen limeade concentrate
- 1/2 cup frozen strawberries
- 1/2 cup ice
- 1 cup coconut water

INSTRUCTIONS:

Place all ingredients into your blender and blend on high for 30 seconds, using the paddle to ensure all ingredients are blended smoothly, enjoy!

BENEFITS:

Coconut water and strawberries are high in potassium. Watermelon is made up mostly of water, combined with the coconut water this is a super hydrating summer time smoothie.

NUTRITION:

| Calories: 145 | Fat: 0g | Carbs: 37g | Protein: 1g |

Chocolate Covered Strawberry Smoothie

Makes One Servings

INGREDIENTS:

- 1 cup frozen strawberries
- 1 cup 0% fat vanilla Greek yogurt
- 1 cup skim milk
- 2 tablespoons cacao or cocoa powder
- 2 medjool dates, pitted

INSTRUCTIONS:

Place all ingredients into your blender and blend on high for 30 seconds, using the paddle to ensure all ingredients are blended smoothly, enjoy!

BENEFITS:

Strawberries are high in fiber, vitamin C, and potassium, they also contain many antioxidants. The yogurt and skim milk provide protein and calcium.

NUTRITION:

Calories: 385   Fat: 2g   Carbs: 58g   Protein: 34g

Chilly Cappaccino Breakfast Smoothie

Makes One Servings

Ingredients:

- 1 cup 0% fat vanilla Greek yogurt
- 1 cup skim milk
- 2 tablespoons instant espresso powder
- 1 tablespoon cacao or cocoa powder
- 2 medjool dates, pitted

Instructions:

Place all ingredients into your blender and blend on high for 30 seconds, using the paddle to ensure all ingredients are blended smoothly, enjoy!

Benefits:

This smoothie is low in fat and high in protein from the yogurt and skim milk. Additionally, it is very high in calcium and the espresso powder will give your morning a kick start.

Nutrition:

| Calories: 316 | Fat: 1g | Carbs: 45g | Protein: 32g |

Banana Date Smoothie:

Makes One Servings

Ingredients:

- 1 large, very ripe banana, frozen
- 1 cup skim milk
- 4 large Medjool dates, pitted

Instructions:

Add all ingredients to your blender and blend on high speed for 30 seconds, using the paddle to ensure all ingredients are blended smoothly, enjoy!

Benefits:

Bananas are high in potassium and tryptophan, an essential amino acid needed for normal growth in infants and nitrogen balance in adults. Dates are a great natural sweetener, they are easy on your blood sugar and help add creaminess to the smoothie. This smoothie is a great post-workout drink!

Nutrition:

Calories: 346   Fat: 1g   Carbs: 80g   Protein: 11g

CREAMY GREEN AVOCADO SMOOTHIE:

Makes One Servings

INGREDIENTS:

- 1/2 medium avocado
- 1 very ripe banana, frozen
- 1/2 cup fresh spinach
- 1/2 cup frozen pineapple chunks
- 1 cup skim milk

INSTRUCTIONS:

Add all ingredients to your blender and blend for 30 seconds, using the paddle to ensure all ingredients are blended smoothly, enjoy!

BENEFITS:

Both avocados and bananas are high in potassium, making this smoothie a great breakfast choice or afternoon pick me up. Avocado is also high in mono saturated fat, a heart friendly fat essential to healthy body function.

NUTRITION:

| Calories: 351 | Fat: 13g | Carbs: 54g | Protein: 13g |

GET YOU GOING SMOOTHIE

Makes One Servings

INGREDIENTS:

- 1/4 cup regular dry oats
- 1 cup vanilla 0% fat Greek yogurt
- 1 cup frozen strawberries
- 1 cup skim milk

INSTRUCTIONS:

Add all ingredients to your blender and mix on high for 30 seconds, use the paddle to make sure all ingredients are blended smoothly, enjoy!

BENEFITS:

Oatmeal is high in fiber which means that it will keep you feeling full until your next meal.
Skim milk and Greek yogurt are both fat free but high in calcium and protein, essential to building and maintaining strong bones.

NUTRITION:

Calories: 339   Fat: 2g   Carbs: 50g   Protein: 34g

RUBY RASPBERRY SMOOTHIE

Makes One Servings

INGREDIENTS:

- 1 cup frozen raspberries
- 1 ruby red grapefruit
- 1 tablespoon chia seeds
- 4 medjool dates, pitted
- 4 ice cubes
- 1/2 cup water

INSTRUCTIONS:

Place frozen raspberries in your blender. Peel grapefruit, remove any large seeds and place half of it into your blender. Add remaining ingredients and blend on high speed for 45 seconds, using the paddle to insure everything is blended evenly, enjoy!

BENEFITS:

Chia seeds are high in protein and healthy omega fats. Medjool dates add creaminess and sweetness to the smoothie without raising your blood sugar the way that white sugar does. Grapefruit is high in vitamin C and raspberries are high in antioxidants.

NUTRITION:

Calories: 325	Fat: 4g	Carbs: 72g	Protein: 7g

SOUPS

Loaded Potato Soup

Ingredients:

- 1 cup chicken broth
- 2 large russet potatoes, peeled and cut into small cubes
- 1 small onion, roughly chopped
- 1 cup whole milk
- ½ cup reduced fat cheddar cheese, shredded
- 1 teaspoon each, salt and pepper
- 1 teaspoon paprika
- 1 teaspoon garlic powder
- For Topping:
- 2 slices bacon, cooked and crumbles
- ¼ cup chives, sliced thin
- 2 tablespoons low-fat sour cream

Instructions:

Place a medium saucepan over medium heat and add chicken broth, potatoes, and onion. Cover and cook for 15 minutes, until potatoes are fork tender. Transfer potato mixture to your blender and add milk, cheese, and seasonings. Blend on high for two minutes, pour soup into two separate bowls and top with bacon, chives, and sour cream, enjoy!

BENEFITS:

This soup is not only delicious but a low calorie version of your favorite loaded baked potato. Milk and cheese add calcium and protein.

NUTRITION:

| Calories: 492 | Fat: 13g | Carbs: 73g | Protein: 22g |

Spicy Tomatillo Soup with Chicken

Makes Two Servings

Ingredients:

- 4 tomatillos
- ¼ cup red onion, chopped
- 1 clove garlic, minced
- ½ cup cilantro
- ½ jalapeño pepper, seeds removed
- 1 ½ cups chicken broth
- 1 teaspoon each, salt and pepper
- 1 cup shredded chicken (canned, boiled, or rotisserie)
- 2 tablespoons light sour cream

Instructions:

Add tomatillos, onion, garlic, cilantro, pepper, broth, and salt and pepper to your blender and mix on high for five minutes. Change speed to low, add in chicken and turn your blender off. Plate and top with fresh sour cream, enjoy!

Benefits:

Tomatillos are a great source of dietary fiber, niacin, potassium and manganese. Niacin helps support your metabolism, cells need it to help convert food to energy. This is a great, tasty low-calorie soup with protein thanks to the shredded chicken.

Nutrition:

Calories: 165	Fat: 3g	Carbs: 6g	Protein: 22g

Roasted Red Pepper Soup

Makes Two Servings

Ingredients:

- 1 tablespoon butter
- 1 small onion, chopped
- 2 large carrots, chopped
- 2 stalks celery, chopped
- 2 cloves garlic, minced
- 1 15.5 ounce jar roasted red peppers, drained and rinsed
- 1 cup vegetable broth
- ¼ cup half and half
- 1 teaspoon each, salt and pepper
- 1 teaspoon garlic powder

Instructions:

Heat a small saucepan over medium heat. Add butter, once melted, add onion carrots, celery, and garlic. Cook, stirring often, until vegetables have softened, about 15 minutes. Once soft, transfer vegetables to your blender and add roasted red peppers, broth, half and half, and seasonings. Mix on high speed for 1 minute, enjoy!

BENEFITS:

Carrots are high in beta-carotene, red peppers are high in vitamins A and C.

NUTRITION:

| Calories: 210 | Fat: 9g | Carbs: 18g | Protein: 2g |

Sweet Potato Bisque

Makes Two Servings

Ingredients:

- 2 large sweet potatoes
- 2 large Roma tomatoes
- 2 cups vegetable broth
- ¼ cup half and half
- 1 teaspoon dried ginger
- ½ teaspoon cinnamon
- 1 teaspoon cayenne pepper
- 1 teaspoon each, salt and pepper

Instructions:

Peirce sweet potatoes with a fork a few time and then microwave for 4 minutes on each side. Let potatoes cool for five minutes and then scoop out from the skin into your blender. Add all remaining ingredients and mix on high for 2 minutes, enjoy!

Benefits:

Sweet potatoes are lower in carbohydrates than traditional potatoes and are high in potassium and vitamin A. This soup is delicious and creamy while remaining low-calorie and low-fat.

Nutrition:

Calories: 175	Fat: 4g	Carbs: 33g	Protein: 4g

Black Bean Soup

Makes Two Servings

INGREDIENTS:

- 1 tablespoon olive oil
- 1 small onion, chopped
- 1 jalapeño pepper, seeded and chopped
- 2 cloves garlic, minced
- 1 can black beans, drained and rinsed
- 1 cup vegetable broth
- ½ cup cilantro
- 1 tablespoon apple cider vinegar
- 1 tablespoon cumin
- 1 teaspoon pepper
- 2 teaspoons garlic powder
- 1 teaspoon oregano

INSTRUCTIONS:

Heat a saucepan over medium heat and add oil, onion, pepper, and garlic. Cook for five minutes and then add beans and broth and cook for an additional five minutes. Transfer to blender, add remaining ingredients and mix on low for 15 seconds, enjoy!

BENEFITS:

This is a great vegan soup as it provides delicious richness and flavor along with protein and fiber to keep you full and satisfied.

NUTRITION:

Calories: 245	Fat: 7g	Carbs: 34g	Protein: 12

Carrot Ginger Soup

Makes Four Servings

INGREDIENTS:

- 1 pound large carrots, peeled
- 1/2 cup chopped onion
- 2 cloves garlic, minced
- 1 inch fresh ginger, minced
- 2 cups vegetable broth

INSTRUCTIONS:

Roughly chop carrots into 1-2 inch pieces and transfer to a large soup pot over medium-high heat. To the pot add the onion, garlic, ginger, and vegetable broth. Once everything comes to a boil, reduce heat to medium-low, cover the pot and cook for 15 minutes. Next, transfer all ingredients to your blender and mix on high for 1 minute, enjoy!

BENEFITS:

Ginger helps to combat nausea and vomiting and can inhibit rhinovirus making this a perfect soup if you are feeling under the weather or fighting a cold.

NUTRITION:

Calories: 62	Fat: 0g	Carbs: 14g	Protein: 1g

BROCCOLI CHEDDAR SOUP

Makes Four Servings

INGREDIENTS:

- 1 cup extra sharp reduced fat cheddar cheese, shredded
- 2 cups milk (1% or 2%)
- 2 1/2 cups fresh broccoli, roughly chopped and washed
- 1/2 cup onion, chopped
- 2 chicken bouillon cubes
- 1 tablespoon garlic powder
- 1 tablespoon fresh or dried thyme
- 2 teaspoons ground black pepper

INSTRUCTIONS:

Place all ingredients into your blender and blend on high for 6 minutes, at this time soup will be cooked and hot, enjoy!

BENEFITS:

Broccoli is high in iron and fiber, it is great for your digestive system and contains antioxidants. The cheese and milk add protein and calcium to this delicious dish.

NUTRITION:

Calories: 157	Fat: 6g	Carbs: 14g	Protein: 14g

Chicken Tortilla Soup

Makes Four Servings

Ingredients:

- 2 cups chicken broth
- 4 tablespoons taco seasoning
- 2 large carrots, roughly chopped
- 1/2 cup chopped onion
- 2 cloves garlic, minced
- 1/2 cup canned diced tomatoes
- 2 stalks celery, rinsed
- 1 large green squash, roughly chopped
- 1 large flour tortilla, cut into thin strips
- 1 tablespoon vegetable oil
- 1/2 cup frozen corn, thawed
- 1 cup shredded chicken (use canned, boiled, or rotisserie
- 1/2 cup fresh cilantro

Instructions:

Add chicken broth, taco seasonings, carrots, onion, garlic, tomatoes, celery, and green squash to your blender and mix on high for 6 minutes. While soup is cooking, place a pan over medium heat, add oil and tortilla strips and cook until strips are crispy and brown, about 5 minutes. Next, turn the high speed switch off, remove the lid plug and drop in the corn, chicken, and cilantro and blend for 5 seconds. Plate soup and top with crispy tortilla strips, enjoy!

BENEFITS:

This soup provides a range of benefits because it is made of a variety of vegetables. Because you are only cooking this soup in your blender, it allows the vegetables to maintain many of the nutrients that often get cooked out when you cook soup for a long period of time on the stove.

NUTRITION:

| Calories: 262 | Fat: 8g | Carbs: 31.5g | Protein: 16g |

Roasted Butternut Squash Soup

Ingredients:

- 1 medium butternut squash (about four cups)
- 1 large green apple
- 1 vidalia onion
- 2 tablespoons olive oil

Makes Four Servings

- 2 cloves garlic, minced
- 1 1/2 cups vegetable broth
- 2 teaspoons ground thyme
- 1 teaspoon each salt and pepper
- 1 teaspoon garlic powder
- 1 teaspoon cinnamon

Instructions:

Preheat oven to 375 degrees. Peel butternut squash and slice into small cubes. Core apple, peel onion, and chop both into quarters. Transfer butternut squash, apples, and onion to a nonstick baking sheet and rub them with olive oil and minced garlic. Bake for 20 minutes and then transfer to your blender. Pour in the vegetable broth and add thyme, salt, pepper, garlic powder, and cinnamon. Mix on high for 45 seconds and enjoy right away or refrigerate and reheat later!

BENEFITS:

One serving of butternut squash has almost 300% of your daily value of vitamin A, essential for eye health. In addition, it is high in vitamin C and low in fat and carbohydrates.

NUTRITION:

Calories: 159	Fat: 7g	Carbs: 25g	Protein: 2g

Cantaloupe Gazpacho

Makes Four Servings

INGREDIENTS:

- 4 cups peeled and chopped cantaloupe (about 1 melon)
- 1/2 large hothouse cucumber, roughly chopped
- 1/4 cup chopped red onion
- 2 tablespoons olive oil
- 1 cup cold filtered water
- 1 teaspoon each, salt and pepper
- Fresh mint for topping

INSTRUCTIONS:

Add cantaloupe, cucumber, red onion, oil, water, and salt and pepper to your blender. Blend the gazpacho on high speed for 30-45 seconds, until the soup reaches a smooth consistency, make sure not to over blend as to avoid heating up the soup. Enjoy right away or chill in the fridge for later, serving with fresh sliced mint.

BENEFITS:

Gazpacho is a cold, raw soup meaning that all of the ingredients retain their vitamins and nutrients. One serving of this gazpacho will provide you with over 100% of your daily value of vitamin A and almost 100% of your daily value of vitamin C.

NUTRITION:

Calories: 133	Fat: 7g	Carbs: 18g	Protein: 2g

Jesse Morgan – FitRecipe.Net

EASY TOMATO BASIL SOUP

Makes Two Servings

INGREDIENTS:

- 1 pound Roma tomatoes
- 2 tablespoons olive oil
- 2 cloves garlic, minced
- 1 small white onion, roughly chopped
- 1 cup vegetable or chicken broth
- 1 cup fresh basil leaves
- 1 teaspoon each, salt and pepper
- 1 teaspoon garlic powder

INSTRUCTIONS:

Wash tomatoes, slice in half, and scoop out the seeds. Set the tomatoes aside, place a small saucepan over medium heat and add the olive oil. Once the oil is hot, add the minced garlic and chopped onion. Cook, stirring often, until the onion and soft and translucent, about 10 minutes. Add the tomatoes to your blender along with the cooked onion and garlic, broth, basil, salt and pepper, and garlic powder. Turn the blender on and mix for two minutes. Enjoy the soup as is or transfer to a saucepan to heat to your preference, enjoy!

Benefits:

Tomatoes are high in vitamin C, A, folic acid, and the antioxidant lycopene. Not only are tomatoes good for your immune system, they fight free radicals through their antioxidant properties. Free radicals can come from stress, a pour diet, lack of exercise, too much exercise, pollution and other things. Free radicals negatively affect normal cell growth and activity.

Nutrition:

Calories: 201	Fat: 14g	Carbs: 19g	Protein: 3g

Potato Leek Soup

> **Makes Two Servings**

INGREDIENTS:

- 2 large leeks
- 2 large russet potatoes
- 2 cloves garlic
- 2 tablespoons olive oil
- 2 cups vegetable or chicken broth
- 1 teaspoon each, salt and pepper

INSTRUCTIONS:

Cut the green portion of the leeks off and discard, you will only want the white parts for this recipe. Chop into large pieces and soak in water, leeks tend to hold onto a lot of dirt so you will want to make sure to wash them thoroughly Peel and rinse potatoes, and cut into small square pieces as you would for mashed potatoes. Mince the garlic and add the olive oil to a medium saucepan over medium heat. Once oil is hot, add your washed leeks and garlic and sauté for four minutes, stirring often. Next, pour your broth into the pan and add your potatoes. Lower heat to medium-low and cover, cook for 15 minutes, until potatoes are fork tender. Next, carefully pour the contents of your saucepan into your blender, add the salt and pepper and place the lid on your blender. Blend for about 30 seconds on high speed, until the soup forms a smooth mixtures, enjoy!

BENEFITS:

Leeks are high in Vitamin K which assists with blood clotting and is essential to strong, healthy bones.

NUTRITION:

| Calories: 345 | Fat: 14g | Carbs: 18g | Protein: 7 |

Fresh Corn Chowder

Makes Two Servings

Ingredients:

- 2 cups fresh corn kernels
- 1 cup whole milk
- 1 yellow bell pepper, roughly chopped and seeded
- ¼ cup fresh cilantro
- 1 teaspoon garlic powder
- 1 teaspoon each, salt and pepper

Instructions:

Add all ingredients to your blender and mix on high for 4 minutes, until hot and steaming. Pour into serving bowls and enjoy!

CREAMY PEA SOUP

Makes Two Servings

INGREDIENTS:

- 1 large red skinned potato
- 2 cups frozen peas, thawed
- ½ cup chopped white onion
- 1 cup vegetable broth
- 1 clove garlic, minced
- 1 teaspoon each, salt and pepper
- 2 tablespoons heavy cream

INSTRUCTIONS:

Wash potato, pierce with a fork and cook in microwave for 3 minutes on each side. Transfer potato to your blender and add peas, onion, broth, garlic, salt and pepper. Blend on high for 5 minutes, reduce speed to low, add heavy cream and then turn off the blender. Pour into bowls and enjoy!

BENEFITS:

Peas are high in protein, potassium, iron, and Vitamins A and C.

NUTRITION:

| Calories: 309 | Fat: 6g | Carbs: 53g | Protein: 11g |

Quick Pumpkin Soup

> Makes Two Servings

Ingredients:

- 1 tablespoon olive oil
- ½ cup chopped onion
- 2 cloves garlic, minced
- 1 cup canned pumpkin puree
- 2 cups chicken or vegetable broth
- 1 teaspoon pumpkin pie seasonings
- 1 teaspoon garlic powder
- ¼ teaspoon cayenne pepper
- 1 teaspoon each, salt and pepper

Instructions:

Heat a small saucepan over medium heat. Once how, add oil, onion, and garlic and cook for two minutes. Transfer onion and garlic to your blender and add remaining ingredients. Mix on high for 2 minutes, until soup is hot, enjoy! This soup is also great topped with a dollop of crème fresh and a few roasted pumpkin seeds.

Benefits:

Pumpkins are a good source of fiber and are high in beta-carotene, essential to eye health. They are also high in potassium and vitamin C. Pumpkins make this soup incredibly rich and creamy without the need for added cream.

Nutrition:

| Calories: 117 | Fat: 7g | Carbs: 14g | Protein: 1g |

DESSERTS

Fresh Mint Chocolate Chip Ice Cream

Makes Two Servings

INGREDIENTS:

- ½ cup whole milk
- ¼ cup sugar
- 2 tablespoons dry milk
- 1 teaspoon vanilla
- 1 teaspoon peppermint extract
- ¼ cup fresh mint leaves (optional, adds flavor and color)
- 2 cups ice
- ¼ cup miniature chocolate chips

INSTRUCTIONS:

Add milk, sugar, vanilla, peppermint, and mint leaves to your blender and blend on high for 15 seconds. Remove lid, add ice, replace lid and blend everything on high for 45 seconds, using the paddle to ensure everything is mixed evenly. Next, turn the blender on low, remove the paddle and pour the chocolate chips into the hole. Mix only until the chocolate chips are evenly distributed, about 5-10 seconds. Enjoy right away or freeze for later!

BENEFITS:

Fresh mint adds a delicious natural mint flavor to this ice cream along with a natural light green color, as opposed to the green food dye used to color most mint ice creams. Whole milk is used in place of cream to keep the fat and calories low. Powdered milk helps to add a rich and creamy texture to this ice cream. This is a great low calorie, low fat treat that is high in protein and calcium.

NUTRITION:

| Calories: 240 | Fat: 6g | Carbs: 40g | Protein: 6g |

Easy Chocolate Raspberry Mousse

Makes Four Servings

Ingredients:

- 1 cup cold heavy cream
- 1 packet sugar-free dark chocolate pudding
- 1 cup fresh raspberries

Instructions:

Add all ingredients to your blender and blend on high until it forms a whipped cream texture, about 25 seconds. Scoop into small serving bowls and enjoy!

Benefits:

By using sugar free pudding in place of traditional chocolate, you get the same flavor without the added calories and sugar.

Nutrition:

Calories: 241	Fat: 20g	Carbs: 10g	Protein: 2g

Hydrating Kiwi Sorbet

Makes Two Servings

Ingredients:

- 8 very ripe kiwis
- 1 cup coconut water

Instructions:

Choose kiwis that are soft to the touch, this means they are slightly overripe and sweet. Peel the kiwis by slicing them in half and scooping them out with a spoon and transfer to a freezer overnight. Once kiwis are frozen, add coconut water and kiwis to your blender and mix for 45 seconds on high, using the paddle to ensure all ingredients are mixed smoothly, enjoy!

Benefits:

Kiwis are very high in Vitamin C, making this sorbet a great immune booster. Coconut water adds a subtle sweetness to the sorbet along with high levels of potassium making this sorbet both refreshing and hydrating.

Nutrition:

Calories: 198	Fat: 2g	Carbs: 40g	Protein: 4g

Vanilla and Green Tea Ice Cream

Makes Four Servings

INGREDIENTS:

- 1 cup whole milk
- 4 cups ice cubes
- 1/2 cup dry milk
- 1/2 cup coconut sugar
- 1 tablespoon pure vanilla extract
- 3 tablespoons match green tea powder

INSTRUCTIONS:

Place all ingredients in your blender and mix on high using paddle to make sure all ingredients blend smoothly for about 45 seconds. Enjoy!

BENEFITS:

Green tea is high in chlorophyll making it a great antioxidant. Coconut sugar is a blood sugar friendly alternative to traditional white sugar. This is a creamy and delicious low-fat alternative to traditional ice cream.

NUTRITION:

| Calories: 167 | Fat: 2g | Carbs: 33g | Protein: 5g |

GINGER PEACH FROZEN YOGURT

Makes Two Servings

INGREDIENTS:

- 2 cups frozen sliced peaches
- 1 tablespoon dried ground ginger*
- 1 cup 0% fat vanilla Greek yogurt
- 1/4 cup skim milk

INSTRUCTIONS:

Remove peaches from freezer and let them sit at room temperature to thaw slightly. Transfer peach slices to your blender along with ginger, Greek yogurt, and skim milk. Blend on high speed for 45 seconds, using the paddle to gently push the peaches into the blade ensuring you get a smooth, evenly blended finished product. Enjoy!

*You can also use a minced 1-inch piece of fresh ginger if you prefer a stronger, fresh ginger flavor.

BENEFITS:

This frozen yogurt is a great alternative to the traditional frozen yogurts found in grocery stores, it has no added sugar and no artificial ingredients. The Greek yogurt adds protein which makes this dessert both a delicious treat and a diet friendly choice.

NUTRITION:

Calories: 142	Fat: 0g	Carbs: 23g	Protein: 14g

Pina Colada Ice Cream

Ingredients:

- ➢ 1 large, very ripe pineapple*
- ➢ 1/4C cream of coconut

Makes Four Servings

Instructions:

Peel of core pineapple, slice into bite-sized pieces and freeze until firm, at least 6-8 hours. Once frozen, remove pineapple from freezer and leave on counter for five minutes, just to soften slightly so it will be easier to mix. Transfer pineapple to your blnender, mix and add 1/4 cup cream of coconut. Blend on high speed for 30 seconds, use the paddle to ensure that all of the pineapple is blended evenly. Enjoy right away or freeze for later.

*You can also use a one pound bag of store bought frozen pineapple.

BENEFITS:

1 serving of pineapple provides you with over 100% of your daily value of vitamin C, which is great for boosting your immune system. Pineapple is also high in B vitamins which promote energy.

NUTRITION:

Calories: 144	Fat: 3g	Carbs: 31g	Protein: 1g

Orange Sorbet

Ingredients:

- 2 pounds fresh oranges
- 1/2 cup coconut sugar
- 1/2 cup water

Makes Four Servings

Instructions:

Peel oranges and place them into your blender, blend on high for 30 seconds. Place a small saucepan over medium heat and add the coconut sugar and water. Cook until the sugar is dissolved, about 2-3 minutes. Add the sugar water into your blender and stir to combine with the orange juice. Pour this orange mixture into ice cube trays and transfer to the freezer. Freeze until solid, about 8 hours. Once frozen, pop the orange ice cubes out of the tray and place them into your blender. Turn the blender on high speed and use the paddle to gently push down the ice cubes. Mix until the ice cubs form a smooth, sorbet like texture, about 45 seconds, enjoy!

BENEFITS:

Oranges are high in vitamin C, an excellent immune system booster. Coconut sugar is a great alternative to traditional white sugar as it does not cause they same spike in blood sugar levels, making it a blood sugar friendly alternative.

NUTRITION:

Calories: 171	Fat: 0g	Carbs: 45g	Protein: 2g

Watermelon Lime Granita

Makes Four Servings

Ingredients:

- 2 limes
- 6 C chopped watermelon
- 1/4C coconut sugar

Instructions:

Zest one of the limes and add the zest to your blender. Slice the two limes in half and squeeze the juice into the blender. Add the watermelon to your blender, along with the coconut sugar and blend everything on high speed for 45 seconds. Transfer watermelon mixture to a large, glass baking dish and freeze for three hours. Remove the dish from the freezer and use a fork to scrape the entire pan so that the watermelon juice looks like shaved ice. Return the pan to the freezer until ready to serve. Once ready to serve, let thaw on the counter for 10-15 minutes and then scrape with a fork again before serving. Enjoy!

Benefits:

Watermelon is a great hot weather treat, it is made mostly of water making it very hydrating In addition watermelon is also high in lycopene and vitamins A and C.

Nutrition:

Calories: 114	Fat: 0g	Carbs: 29g	Protein: 1g

Strawberry Frozen Yogurt

Makes Two Servings

INGREDIENTS:

- 1 cup 0% fat strawberry or vanilla Greek yogurt
- 2 cups frozen strawberries

INSTRUCTIONS:

Add yogurt to the bottom of your blender and then add strawberries on top. Mix on high speed for 45 seconds, gently use the paddle to press the strawberries down and ensure everything is mixed evenly, enjoy!

BENEFITS:

This is a great low-calorie, fat-free dessert; the yogurt adds calcium and protein. Strawberries have are high in antioxidants and vitamin C making them cancer fighting immune boosters.

NUTRITION:

Calories: 114	Fat: 0g	Carbs: 17g	Protein: 12g

Homemade Strawberry Sauce

Makes Four Servings

Ingredients:

- ½ cup water
- ½ cup coconut sugar
- 2 cups fresh strawberries, washed with tops cut off

Instructions:

Heat a small pan over medium heat and all the water, sugar, and strawberries. Cook for 10 minutes, until sugar is melted and strawberries have softened. Pour the strawberry mixture into your blender and mix on high for 10 seconds. Enjoy over fresh ice cream or cake!

Benefits:

Strawberries are high in antioxidants and Vitamin C, they are a great cancer fighting immune booster. Coconut sugar adds a blood sugar friendly sweetness.

Nutrition:

Calories: 114	Fat: 0g	Carbs: 30g	Protein: 1g

Blueberry Lemon Pound Cake

Makes Eight Servings

INGREDIENTS:

- 1 1/4 cups 0% fat lemon Greek yogurt
- ¼ cup skim milk
- 2 large eggs
- 1 stick of butter
- ¾ cup sugar
- Juice and zest of 2 lemons
- 1 ½ cups flour
- 1 teaspoon baking powder
- 1 cup fresh or frozen blueberries

INSTRUCTIONS:

Preheat oven to 325 degrees. Place yogurt, milk, eggs, butter, sugar, and lemon zest and juice in your blender and mix on high for 30 seconds. Add flour and baking powder to a large mixing bowl and stir to combine. Add the wet ingredients to the mixing bowl and stir well, gently stir in the blueberries and pour into a greased and floured loaf pan. Bake until golden, about 1 hour. Let cake cool before removing from pan and enjoy!

BENEFITS:

Blueberries are high in antioxidants. By replacing half of the butter with Greek yogurt, this cake retains its moisture without all the extra fat and calories.

Nutrition:

| Calories: 297 | Fat: 9g | Carbs: 43.5g | Protein: 11g |

BANANA SOFT SERVE ICE CREAM

Makes Two Servings

INGREDIENTS:

➢ 4 very ripe large bananas, frozen

INSTRUCTIONS:

Take frozen bananas out of freezer and allow to sit on counter for 5 minutes, to soften slightly. Transfer pineapple to your blnender and mix on high for 30 seconds, using the paddle to ensure everything mixes evenly. Use an ice cream scoop to scoop out your ice cream and enjoy!

*You can easily change up this recipe by keeping bananas as the base and adding other flavors such as pineapple, mango, mixed berries, ginger, etc.

BENEFITS:

This is a great alternative to traditional ice cream as it is low-fat and vegan. This ice cream is just as creamy as traditional ice cream and has the added benefit of potassium from the bananas.

NUTRITION:

Calories: 200	Fat: 1g	Carbs: 54g	Protein: 3g

Mango Chili Pops

Makes Four Pops

INGREDIENTS:

- 2 cups fresh sliced mango
- 2 teaspoons chili powder
- ½ cup coconut water

INSTRUCTIONS:

Add all ingredients to your blender and blend on high for 15 seconds. Pour into a set of four Popsicle molds and freeze for 4-6 hours, enjoy!

*You can find plastic Popsicle molds at most grocery and home stores. You can also make your own Popsicle mold by using a small paper cup and a Popsicle stick.

BENEFITS:

Mango is high in potassium and vitamins A and C.

NUTRITION:

| Calories: 65 | Fat: 0g | Carbs: 17g | Protein: 0g |

COCONUT LIME SORBET

> **Makes Two Servings**

INGREDIENTS:

- ½ cup fresh lime juice
- 2 tablespoons fresh lime zest
- ¼ cup coconut sugar
- 1 cup water
- ¼ cup full-fat coconut milk

INSTRUCTIONS:

Heat a small saucepan over medium heat, add the lime juice, zest, coconut sugar and water. Allow too cook, stirring constantly, until the sugar has dissolved, about 3 minutes. Next, stir in the coconut milk and pour the lime mixture into ice cube trays and freeze. Once frozen, remove ice cube trays from freeze, pop out the lime ice cubes and transfer to your blender. Mix on high for 45 seconds, using paddle to ensure everything mixes evenly, enjoy right away or freeze for later!

BENEFITS:

Limes contain citrate which is thought to reduce the risk of kidney stones, they are also high in potassium and vitamin C. The coconut sugar adds a blood sugar friendly sweetness while the coconut milk adds delicious flavor and keeps the sorbet scoopable even when refrozen.

NUTRITION:

Calories: 134	Fat: 3g	Carbs: 30g	Protein: 1g

Homemade Healthy Truffles

Makes Eighteen Servings

INGREDIENTS:

- 1 cup walnuts
- 10 Medjool dates, pitted
- 2 tablespoons coconut oil (use refined coconut oil if you don't want the coconut flavor)
- 2 tablespoons cacao powder (or cocoa powder)
- 2 tablespoons agave nectar
- ¼ cup miniature chocolate chips
- ½ cup puffed rice cereal

INSTRUCTIONS:

Place walnuts and pitted dates into your blender and blend on high until they form a paste, about 45 seconds. Next, add coconut oil, cacao powder, and agave nectar and blend on high for an additional 15 seconds to ensure everything is well mixed. Scoop the mixture out of your blender and place into a large mixing bowl. Mix in the miniature chocolate chips and rice cereal and then use your hands to form into small round balls. This recipe will make about 18 truffles, depending on how large you choose to make them. Refrigerate for at least one hour to allow your truffles to harden up and enjoy!

BENEFITS:

These truffles are perfect for anyone who is trying to eat healthy but can't get rid of their chocolate cravings. Both walnuts and coconut oil are high in essential, heart friendly fats. Dates make these truffles creamy while adding a blood sugar friendly sweetness.

NUTRITION:

| Calories: 103 | Fat: 6.5g | Carbs: 11g | Protein: 1.5g |